The Art of Manipulation

Powerful Techniques on How to Influence Human Behavior, Effectively Deal with People, and Get the Results You Want

Antony Felix

Your Free Gift

As a way of thanking you for the purchase, I'd like to offer you a complimentary gift:

- **5 Pillar Life Transformation Checklist:** This short book is about life transformation, presented in bit size pieces for easy implementation. I believe that without such a checklist, you are likely to have a hard time implementing anything in this book and any other thing you set out to do religiously and sticking to it for the long haul. It doesn't matter whether your goals relate to weight loss, relationships, personal finance, investing, personal development, improving communication in your family, your overall health, finances, improving your sex life, resolving issues in your relationship, fighting PMS successfully, investing, running a successful business, traveling etc. With a checklist like this one, you can bet that anything you do will seem a lot easier to implement until the end. Therefore, even if you don't continue reading this book, at least read the one thing that will help you in every other aspect of your life. [Grab your copy now by clicking/tapping here](http://bit.ly/2fantonfreebie) or simply enter http://bit.ly/2fantonfreebie into your browser. Your life will never be the same again (if you implement what's in this book), I promise.

PS: I'd like your feedback. If you are happy with this book, please leave a review on Amazon.

Introduction

'The ability to influence people without irritating them is the most profitable skill you can learn.'- Napoleon Hill

Do you often find it hard to convince your friends to do something you want? Is it difficult for you to explain your viewpoint to your boss and positively influence him/her so he/she agrees to put you as the team leader? Do you experience a tough time making your spouse/partner understand and accept your opinion and have them on board to pursue an idea? Do people see you as more annoying than influential? Do you wish to have a superpower that makes you come off as an influential and charismatic individual whom everybody loves and is always ready to listen to?

If you answered yes to these questions, it is likely you currently have poor communication and manipulative skills and are yet to learn the art of convincing and inspiring people. This important skill is crucial if you wish to be successful in your personal relationships, career, professional life, social circle and any aspect of life that involves dealing with people.

It can be quite tricky to effectively deal with people, help them come on the same page as you and convince them to do what you wish, but it is nonetheless doable and if you committedly work towards the fulfillment of this goal, you can achieve it.

The Art of Manipulation

Influencing, inspiring and persuading people is an art, which needs to be treated like one. Instead of wanting to control everyone as if they are your puppets so they dance to your tune, your goal needs to be to positively influence and lead them. Yes, you can have ulterior motives that you wish to have fulfilled, but if they are positive and you do not intend to harm anyone, you are on the right track and there is nothing wrong with making others agree with you. However, how can you achieve that?

The answers to that question are locked within this book. This book is a handy guide that provides you with detailed insight into the importance of influencing people while providing you with actionable, helpful and effective techniques to effectively deal with them and get your desired results every time.

Table of Contents

Your Free Gift _____ 2

Introduction _____ 3

Chapter 1: Why Learn To Influence Others _ 7

    Benefits of Influencing People _____ 9

Chapter 2: Comprehend The Decision Cycle
_____ 13

Chapter 3: Work On Your Body Language And Speaking Style _____ 18

    Improve Your Body Language _____ 20

    Observe the Body Language of Others _____ 23

    Your Speaking Style _____ 25

Chapter 4: Build Trust And Be Consistent In Your Efforts _____ 31

    Build Faith _____ 31

    Carry Out all Your Efforts Consistently _____ 34

Chapter 5: More Effective Techniques To Influence Others _____ 40

    Be Aware of Your BATNA _____ 43

Conclusion _____ 48

Do You Like My Book & Approach To Publishing? _____ **49**

1: First, I'd Love It If You Leave a Review of This Book on Amazon._____49

2: Check Out My Emotional Mastery Books ____49

3: Grab Some Freebies On Your Way Out; Giving Is Receiving, Right? _____50

Chapter 1: Why Learn To Influence Others

The most influential business people, collaborators, entrepreneurs, innovators and leaders across the globe have one thing in common, which is also the most important characteristic that facilitates them in accomplishing their goals and bringing the change they wish to see in the society; their ability to connect with people and win them over. Influencing people is a skill that never goes out of fashion and is always required to live a successful, meaningful life.

Let us establish what influencing people means and then move on to discussing the many reasons you need to work on to inculcate this skill in yourself.

What Influencing Others Means

Influence refers to having the power that leaves an important and lasting effect on something or someone. When you influence someone, you try to change that person in an indirect way. The influence can be both, positive or negative. At times, someone trying to influence someone does not have the intention to do so, but quite often, this is done with the motive to achieve a certain goal and enjoy some benefit.

When you try to win over someone or influence him/her, you have the intention to make that person do any or all of the following:

- Agree to do you a certain favor

- Fulfill a certain demand
- Help you out with a task
- Abandon their viewpoint and accept yours
- Accept your ideas and work as you want to
- Do not object to your beliefs and acknowledge them
- Respect your wishes and abide by them
- Willingly and happily follow your instructions without nurturing any ill feelings about it
- Hold you in great reverence and see you as an authority and influential figure
- Shower affection and care for you
- Be ready to hang out with you
- Engage cordially with you and share a harmonious relationship with you

When someone does one or more of the aforementioned things, it is likely because you have been able to effectively influence him because of your strong and charismatic personality.

Your goal needs to be to win people over instead of trying to control them. When you do the latter, you are not able to sustain that power over people for a long time because eventually, they become aware of the manipulation and often end up feeling that they are being mistreated. When this realization dawns upon them, they are likely to break free from your control and abandon you.

As opposed to this, if you focus more on winning people over and positively influencing them, you can have your cake and eat it too. When you do not try to manipulate people, just slowly and gradually build the point where you can easily convince them without harming their emotional wellbeing and self-esteem, deal with them in a manner that they feel happy while agreeing with you on everything, you can easily achieve all your goals, and sustain happy relationships as well.

Let us now look at some of the benefits you can enjoy by learning the art of influencing others:

Benefits of Influencing People

Influencing and positively manipulating people, enables you to enjoy the following benefits:

- Make loved ones agree to accept your decisions: In a family, there are many situations when you have to make tough decisions for the entire family. If at that point, your loved ones do not agree with you, it can be quite a problem for you. However, if you know how to deal with them and influence them, you can easily make them agree with the decision you make.

- Avoid intense arguments: You are likely to encounter some conflict in your relationships or even at work. In all these situations, you need to know how to easily sway and convince others so that you avoid arguments and achieve your goal without coming off as a the controlling person.

- Utilize Good Opportunities: Opportunities often knock your door disguised as threats or obstacles. If you can perceive those threats as opportunities and know how to turn things around, you need to be able to communicate the same message to the other people involved in that situation too. This is how you can avail good opportunities and move further in life.

- Achieve Success in Business: Your business growth and success is largely dependent on the performance of your entire team. To make sure all the team members put in their best effort and work towards the company's benefit, you need to be able to positively influence them first.

- Landing a Good Job: If you know how to influence people, you can easily apply the trick on your interviewers, give a terrific job interview and land the job of your dreams.

- Discipline and Raise Your Kids the Way You Want: Raising kids is a humungous responsibility, one that comes with many challenges. You need to ensure you discipline them, take care of their emotional and physical development and wellbeing, and be fun loving, laid back, appreciative and supportive too. Doing all of that at the same time while making sure you do not overly spoil your babies is a tough one, but definitely doable especially if you know how to influence people and sway them successfully.

- Enjoy a Large Social Network: If you are good at influencing people, you are likely to have quite a nice, big social network full of people who will help you out in the hour of need.

- Become an Influential Leader: Leadership is a skill that not everyone possesses, but is definitely one that you can work on. If you know how to control and influence people without negatively affecting their wellbeing, you can effectively lead them and make them pay heed to all your commands.

- Create a Positive Impact on the Society: One of our innate needs is to create an impact on the society, which you can easily achieve if you know how to influence people and make them understand your viewpoint. You can help them unleash their potential, explore it and use it for the betterment of the society.

Additionally, being able to influence people helps you create harmony in every relationship you share with someone, be it one in a professional capacity or a completely personal one.

Now that you know all the reasons why it is important to develop this skill, let us move on to discussing the techniques you can employ to become an influential person.

Chapter 2: Comprehend The Decision Cycle

Each one of us moves through the decision cycle when deciding something. The decision cycle comprises of 5 major predictable stages, which eventually lead you to make a certain decision which can be desired or even undesired. To be able to successfully influence people, you need to have an understanding of the decision cycle and then be able to identify the stage someone is on as well as the stage you are on so you can use the appropriate techniques and convince him/ her.

1. **Identify the Need and a Decision that Needs to be Made**

This is the first stage of the decision making cycle when someone realizes he/she has a need for something and has to make a certain decision. At this stage, you need to be clear about the decision you wish to take so you take the right step forward and can influence the people involved in the decision effectively.

For instance, if you are being offered a great job, but you have to move to another state, you need to decide what will be the most appropriate decision for you and your family. Only then can be clear on the decision you wish to take that you can easily influence others too. If you are confused about it, you are quite likely to feel double minded and may not be able to convince someone else as well.

2. Collect Enough Relevant Information

At this stage, you need to gather as much information as possible regarding the decision you wish to take so you can be sure of it and reach a more informed conclusion. Continuing with the earlier example of moving to another state to pursue a job, you need to gather information on the living expenses in that new state, education expenses of kids and other different factors that entail living there so that you can assess the pros and cons of shifting there and those of living in your current state. Once you have enough data, you can make the right decision for yourself and others involved in the decision.

When it comes to influencing someone who is on this stage, you need to present him/her with enough influential data so he/she is convinced of your decision. For instance, if you fear your partner may not agree to move to another state, you need to convince him/her by presenting him with all the evidences of how life will be better for your family there.

Similarly, if you wish for your friends to agree on something as simple as watching your choice of movie, collect as much information as you can on how that is the best movie to watch that night and how it will be exciting for everyone. In this scenario, the decision is that of watching a movie and the next step is to pick one. If your friends have agreed on watching a movie, you now need to supply them with the right kind of information to convince them to watch a film you want.

3. Identifying Different Alternatives Available and Evaluating Each

As you collect sufficient information to support your decision, you also need to start looking for different alternatives of that choice. This ensures that you make an informed decision instead of jumping for the first thing that catches your fancy.

When you present a certain solution or option to anybody, you would like to convince them to do a certain act and he/she is likely to look for any substitutes available for that option. Your job at this stage is to stay calm and instead of directly telling them how seeking alternatives is not a healthy approach, provide them with substitutes that aren't as good as your choice. Also, you can share the cons of the different alternatives they pick so they ultimately agree to do what you want.

For example, if you want your partner to go out on a picnic with you instead of a mountain hike that he/she is interested in, ask him/her to list down all the pros and cons of both the choices. You can also add in a splash of emotion and tell him/her of how sick you got the last time you went for a hike. As you do that, ensure that you do not make up any excuses, stories or false cons associated with his/her option. Instead, genuinely point out all the reasons why your choice is better.

4. Making a Choice

Once all the different options have been weighed against one another, you and the others involved in the decision are ready to reach a conclusion. When someone reaches this stage, you need to stay as poised as possible and make sure you keep your facial expressions as calm as possible. You must not flinch, twitch or make any expression that makes the other person feel uncomfortable or that his/her choice/decision is not good enough.

However, you also need to stick to your stance and make it clear that you feel it is the best decision for everyone. If you believe your team should select a certain marketing strategy that involves using social media instead of spending a hefty amount of money on billboard advertisement, state it clearly. If you are in a position to make the final call, do so. If, however, you are not in that position and have to somehow accept the decision that everyone agrees to make, do so gracefully without budging from the stance. When the time is right and others experience a setback due to their decision, inform them politely of how you suggested differently and that they should try what you suggested.

5. Review the Final Decision and Any Consequences Faced

This is the final stage of the process when you analyze the decision that was taken and assess whether or not it worked out well in your favor. If the decision failed to meet the need that was identified in the start, you need to take another decision. If you had agreed to do what the other person wanted, but the decision did not turn out to be beneficial, clearly paint the consequences to that person. It is likely they would now agree to do what you want.

A very effective technique to influence others is to let them have their way first especially if you are sure it would backfire. Once the outcome is not even, close to what they expect, you can gently barge in, rub in the fact that you had made a different suggestion and now is the time to try that out. The other person is likely to feel remorseful then and easily agree to what you want. Since he/she feels sorry for making the wrong decision, the likelihood of him/her agreeing to your decisions is quite high the next time around.

Following the decision making cycle and trying different strategies to sway the person at different stages of the cycle is one of the many ways to influence people. Let us now learn about using body language to manipulate others.

Chapter 3: Work On Your Body Language And Speaking Style

Before moving on to discussing any more strategies, it is crucial to teach you the importance of working on your body language and speaking style. If these two elements are not right and effective, no other technique to influence others will work.

Let me discuss the significance of these two tools followed by strategies to improve them.

Body Language

About 80% of the communication you have with others is through your body language, which encompasses your facial expressions, postures, hand gestures, eye movements, use of space and touching different things/body parts with your body.

Without uttering any word, you can easily communicate your confidence, feelings and emotions to others. If you wish to come off as an influential person, you need to keep your body language as effective as possible so you are perceived as an authority figure and are held in utmost respect by others.

Just like your body language speaks volumes about your thoughts, feelings and confidence, that of others around you does the same. While you need to pay attention to structuring your body language the right way so you come off as a strong, confident, charismatic and pleasant individual, you also need to closely observe the body language of all those you wish to influence so you can then target them appropriately using different strategies.

For instance, if you are pitching your business idea to a group of interested investors, and one of them seems puzzled which is evident through the twitching of his eyes or how he keeps pursing his lips, it is possible he is interested in your idea, but needs more information to convince him. At this point, you need to illustrate your in-depth knowledge of the problem and talk to him in detail about how your idea and business will solve a particular problem faced by the target audience.

Similarly, if a friend shares an idea with you and asks you for your input; however, you can clearly see how unconfident she is on her idea by the shrugging of her shoulders and the dullness in her eyes, it is time to give her a good suggestion and reinforce it by providing enough evidence so she agrees to do what you want.

To ensure every strategy you try with someone ends up winning that person over, you need to pay attention to both your body language and that of others.

Here is what you need to do.

Improve Your Body Language

Here are some things you must work on to build powerful and persuasive body language.

- Right Posture: Whether you are standing or sitting, your head must be held high, chin should point slightly upwards, shoulders need to be open and broad while the spine must be straight. While standing, keep your feet at hip distance apart, your pelvis should be open, legs must not shake and arms should be on your side. Body positions with these stances are known as 'high power body poses' and according to Harvard researcher Amy Cuddy's research, they increase your testosterone levels, which is a hormone associated with self-confidence and enthusiasm. Hence, when you engage in these poses, you feel self-assured and calm, and are able to influence others better. The opposite of high power poses are 'low power poses' which are all the poses wherein you have a hunched back, slouched shoulders, chin tilted downwards, limbs closed and head held downwards. Such poses exhibit your lack of confidence on a certain matter to others. Remember, if you come off as an unconfident person, those around you are quite likely not to pay heed to your suggestions and dismiss your ideas. If you are not confident about your ideas, how do you suppose someone else to buy into them? To ensure that does not happen, adopt the right body posture.

- Eye Contact: Your eye contact is another tool that gives away your confidence or a lack of it. If you are constantly moving your gaze away from someone and cannot look him/her in the eye, either you are shying from that person, are unconfident about yourself, or are scared due to some reason. All of this is likely to go against you if you are trying to win someone over especially if it is someone you share a professional relationship with. When conversing with someone, you must maintain direct eye contact with him/ her so your anxiety even if there is any is not exhibited through your eyes. When talking to someone on a one-on-one basis, pick a spot slightly above your listener's eyes and gently focus on it. You need to hold eye contact at that point or even directly in your listener's eyes for 4 to 5 seconds after every 30 to 40 seconds. On breaking the eye contact, gently glance to his/her side before continuing with your gaze. While looking away, do so very gently as darting your eyes may make you appear shy. Remember, not to look at the floor, as it is a sign of nervousness and may make it difficult for you to influence your listener. Every time you start saying something, make direct eye contact with him/her and keep your gaze as gentle as possible. Remember to maintain eye contact about 50% of the time when you speak and around 70 to 80% of the times, when you are listening to the other person as that makes you appear as a keen listener, which the other person is going to love and appreciate about you making it easier for you to influence him. If, you are speaking to more than one person at once, do not take the entire group as one person, but try to initiate individual conversations with different people in the group, one at a time. Talk to the entire group, but maintain eye contact with one person at a time. After you have maintained eye contact with someone for a couple of minutes, choose another person.

- Smile: A nice, hearty smile speaks volume about your sincerity and cordial behavior. When conversing with someone, make sure to flash a nice smile at your listener. Things said with a sweet smile melt the heart of others easily so when you speak to someone, do so with a pleasant smile on your face. Remember to smile at your listener occasionally to send pleasant vibes out to him/her.

- Do Not Practice Gestures that Convey Wrong Messages to Your Listener: There are certain body poses and gestures that convey wrong and inappropriate messages to your listeners, which is why you should refrain from practicing them. For instance, if you are constantly biting your lip, that may mean you are hiding something, are extremely nervous, or are disturbed. If your listeners acknowledge your frustration, they are quite likely not to lean towards you as you hope to. Also, never cover your face while speaking to someone as it is perceived as a sign of dishonesty and is likely to make you appear as a dishonest person to others.

- Pace Around: If you are walking while talking to someone, calmly pace around and take firm strides. Your legs should not tremble as you walk and you need to keep your gait as confident as possible.

- Make Confident Gestures when Needed: During your conversations, make confident hand gestures whenever needed. Make a fist pump to motivate others, thump your fist on the table to stress on something and give your listener a thumbs up to appreciate him/her. Positive and confident hand gestures complement your talk well making it easier for you to influence others.

Observe the Body Language of Others

The different body language cues of those around you can give you valuable information about them and their behavior. Here are some cues you should look out for when interacting with and trying to manipulate people.

- Crossed legs and arms: If you see someone with arms crossed over their chest or crossed legs, it is likely they are angry, defensive or frustrated. With such people, you need to be compassionate and make them feel comfortable prior to bringing up an idea or topic you want their consent on. If you see your boss sitting with crossed arms and you are going to ask him for a 10-day leave, cordially ask him if everything is okay and offer to help. If he does share his trouble with you, do what you can do to ease his pain and then bring up your demand. He is likely to agree to it then.

- Distance and leaning: People lean towards people and things they like and lean away from all those they do not really like. If you see someone leaning towards something, understand he/she is interested in it so bring up that thing in your conversation. Also, if someone leans towards you during a conversation, it is likely he/she likes you and you then need to sustain that interest by talking about things he/she likes. In case, someone you wish to influence leans away from you, focus on what interests him/her and incorporate that in your conversation.

- Biting lips: If someone is licking or biting their lips or picking their cuticles, it is likely he/she is under pressure and is trying to calm his/herself down. When you see someone doing that, gently ask him/her if everything is okay and express your concern. If he/she refuses to discuss it further, leave the topic right away and bring up something else while encouraging him/her to share his/her input on the topic. Soon enough he/she will understand your concern and talk about their problem with you.

- Hiding hands: If you see someone with his/her hands in his/her lap or pocket, or hands behind his/her back, it is likely they are trying to hide something from you. In that case, indirectly ask him/her if everything is okay and then carry some research on your own. You need to tactfully tackle the matter so the other person eventually shares his/ her stuff with you without doubting your intentions.

As you work on your body language, you also need to pay attention to your speaking style and the voice projection so you speak in an influential manner and are able to get the desired outcome of the different influential and manipulative tactics you employ with others.

Your Speaking Style

Here are some things you must work on to persuade others while speaking to them.

- Moderate Tone: Make sure your tone is neither too loud nor too hushed when speaking. An extremely loud tone makes you come off as an aggressive person, which is likely to repel others. Naturally, when people see you as an angry soul who does not know how to respect others, they are likely not to become drawn to you let alone listen to you. Speaking in a very low tone may make you appear as a soft-spoken and cordial individual, but will not help you much in influencing others. If people cannot hear you clearly, they will not understand you. Also, often a hushed tone is seen as a symbol of a lack of confidence and that is always a deal breaker when it comes to being influenced. Your tone needs to be moderate so when you speak, you come off as a poised individual who is sure of what he/she is speaking and knows how to regulate his/her emotions. When people see you as someone calm, they easily discuss their viewpoints with you and the more information you have on others, the better you can influence them. That said, it is important to raise your voice when making a point so others know that you stand for what you believe in and things that you perceive as important and crucial.

- Reiterate an Important Point: When you make an important point, reiterate it a few times in front of your listener. This does two things: first, it makes the other person become more aware of your viewpoint and understand how that belief is important to you. Secondly, when you repeat a certain suggestion, you reinforce it in your subconscious as well as that of others. If you keep saying how you think feminism rocks and present the viewpoints with evidence and respect, you will make the other person become more open to it as well.

- Speak Clearly: Mumbling is a huge sign of a lack of confidence and a practice that will not help you influence anybody much. When speaking to someone, do so very clearly so others can easily understand whatever you say.

- Mimic the Style of the Other Person: Deep down, all of us have an inbuilt need of being connected to the other person and finding some sort of common ground with them. You need to leverage this innate need and use it to influence others. When conversing with someone, pick any prominent cue related to their speech such as their style of speaking, the way they pronounce a certain word, or how they repeat a certain phrase and mimic it yourself. Do it very casually and in a manner that the other person does not feel offended and within a little while, you will observe him/her becoming more comfortable in your presence, and easily sharing his/her things with you.

- Rephrase Things as Many Times as Needed: Oftentimes, it so happens that you are unable to convey your message as desired and it ends up coming off as something else entirely. You may just be asking someone to be attentive in his or her work, but he or she may end up thinking that you are ridiculing them. When you talk to someone, you need to be as cordial as possible especially if you want to influence someone. On other occasions, such as when you are trying to explain your viewpoint, simplify your message as much as you can, and if the need arises, rephrase it countless times without letting your agitation appear in your tone.

- Breathe Properly while Talking: When you breathe quite shallowly in the chest instead of doing so deeply in the abdomen, your voice is likely to sound jittery and weaker. Yes, it can be very tough to breathe very deeply when you are undergoing stress, but by taking deep and calm breaths, you improve the quality and depth of your voice; you sound more confident, calmer and poised, which makes it easier for you to influence others.

- Keep Your Focus Straight: Try to be clear on the agenda of your conversation and speech when initiating it so you keep it in sight and keep bringing up that topic throughout the conversation.

- Ask Questions: When talking to someone, do not only focus on saying things and presenting your viewpoints to others. Instead, ask more questions especially related to the viewpoints of the other person. If someone is talking about his childhood, ask more questions about it and how that affected him. If someone brings up the topic of consumerism, take interest in it and ask questions. This makes the other person feel how keen you are in his/her talk and makes him/her feel drawn towards you. When the other person starts leaning towards you, he/she starts to listen to you more and pay heed to it as well.

- Listen Attentively: As important as it is to speak influentially and present your viewpoint clearly in front of the other person, it is equally important to keenly and attentively listen to him/her as well. Give the other person equal chance to speak and when he/she speaks, do not interrupt him/her at all even if he/she says something you completely disagree with and reject. You need to patiently listen to his/her viewpoint and let him/her explain it in detail. Maintain direct and subtle eye contact with him/ her while he/she speaks and pay complete attention to him by ensuring you do not fidget with your watch or keep checking your phone. Just keep looking at your listener, nod in places to show your agreement when you need to and keep your facial expressions as calm as possible even when you feel like flinching because you disapprove of what he/she says. The more interest you take in his/her chat, the keener you will appear, which will make him/her respect and admire you even more. All of us have an innate need to be heard and speak about our feelings, and desperately need a keen listening ear to which we can pour our heart out. Unfortunately, this remains only a wish for many of us, which increases that yearning inside us to be heard and appreciated. If you can be that one person for others who can listen to them and shower attention onto them, they will love and revere you more. Often people show respect to others by paying heed to their demands so it is likely they will listen to you more and do as you want.

- Stay Hydrated: The quality and pitch of your voice plays a huge role in helping you influence others and one of the other factors that it is dependent on is how hydrated you are. If you are well hydrated, your vocal cords have the right amount of moisture making you sound clear and your tone smooth. However, if you have been consuming more soda, wine and coffee instead of water, your voice will lack the moisture it needs to sound clear. The vocal cords in men vibrate around 120 times/ second and around 200 times/ second in women which means you need to provide your throat with enough moisture to keep it well lubricated so you do not sound hoarse while speaking and speak fluently to charm others.

Let us move on to the next chapter and figure out some more techniques that can assist you in influencing others.

Chapter 4: Build Trust And Be Consistent In Your Efforts

If someone does not trust you and you are not consistent in your efforts, you will always struggle to build good rapport with people and influence them as you wish to. Naturally, if someone cannot bring him/herself up to the point to place his/her faith in you maybe because you keep shifting in the way you treat him/ her, or because you do not come off as an authentic person, he/she will not be drawn towards you and when someone is not attracted to you, he/she will not listen to you either.

You obviously do not want that, right. To ensure you achieve your motive in influencing others, you must do two more things. Let us talk about them in depth here.

Build Faith

Trust is by far the most important element you need to work on when interacting with others so you can then leverage its power and control others exactly how you wish to. If you cannot bring yourself close to someone you do not trust and are likely to reject everything they say, how do you propose that someone else will bring him or herself to do the same with you if they cannot bring an ounce of trust in the relationship they share with you.

As difficult as it seems, trust is actually not that difficult to build. You do a few things right and you can easily make someone put all their confidence in you. Two of those techniques are to listen intently to the other person when he/she speaks and ask questions when talking to him/her. You can do a number of things to achieve this:

- Be Authentic: If you are not genuine in your behavior with others, they will only distrust you. For someone to rely on you, you need to come off as an honest, sincere and authentic person who practices what he/she preaches. If you say you are a person of principles, show that as well. If you portray yourself as a punctual person, always be on time. If you struggle with being honest, but want to inculcate that character trait, accept your mistakes and sincerely exhibit the fact that you struggle with establishing credibility. This may make it a little tough for someone to trust you, but he/she will appreciate your honesty and the fact that you are being upfront about your problem, which will only draw him/her closer to you. Whoever you are as a person, accept and acknowledge it, and portray just that. If you are aware of any of your shortcomings and you know that can make it hard for someone to trust and like you, work on overcoming that drawback to become a better person. Also, list down your positive traits and try to highlight them as much as you can in your personality. If you are a fun, easygoing person, portray yourself as exactly that. Try to be as laid back and engaging with others as you can and do so genuinely so your lighter side comes out in the limelight and draws others towards you.

- Don't Go Back on Your Words: To appear as a trustworthy individual, you need to keep your promises and always abide by what you say. If you commit to something or someone, never go back on your words and fulfill that promise and commitment no matter how little or big it is. Charisma is not just exuded by the way you dress up, walk and speak, it is a mixture of a score of things of which one is to establish trust by fulfilling even your littlest of commitments. If you have committed to your boss to pick up certain documents from the bank even if it is not one of your official duties, do so because that is how he/she will trust you more and then give you the power to influence him/her.

- Be There for People: If you are not there for people in the hour of need especially if you are the one they solely rely on or if the fulfillment of their need is directly dependent on you, you will never win over their trust. You need to be there for others to show them you care enough for them. So if you wish to influence friends and one of them calls you at 4am due to an emergency, do not question them and meet them as soon as possible. When you prove to be there for people, you will eventually win them over and influence them.

- Show Love, Care and Concern: Additionally, shower your love, concern and affection on people you wish to control and live, as you want. Whether it is your business partner, you would like to manipulate or your kids who do not pay heed to your commands, you need to create the foundation of love, trust and care in the relationships you share with them. Keep telling your kids how much you love them and do so genuinely. It may take you a while to get there, but there will come a point when they will love you back. Similarly, if you keep showing your concern to your business partner and take interest in his/her life, you will bring him/her to the point where he/she trusts you blindly and is ready to be indirectly influenced by you.

An important rule to make all these tactics work is to do them consistently. Consistency is indeed the key to success and this applies to every aspect of life.

Carry Out all Your Efforts Consistently

'Foolish consistency is the hobgoblin of little minds.'- Ralph Waldo Emerson

Showing consistency means that you need to align your actions with your core beliefs and stated intentions. Therefore, if you wish for people to trust you, you need to be consistent in all your actions and those must be lined up with your beliefs and intentions. Like Robert Cialdini, the author of 'Influence: The Psychology of Persuasion' states, 'Once we have made a choice or taken a stand, we will encounter personal and interpersonal pressures to behave consistently with that commitment. Those pressures will cause us to respond in ways that justify our earlier decision.'

The pressure of the society on us to conform to something we proclaim does help us stay consistent in our efforts towards a certain goal, which is why experts advise you to make a certain goal public so everyone keeps you accountable to it. You need to be consistent in your own efforts and you need to know the art of leveraging the habit of being consistent in others as well.

In his book, Cialdini explains this by illustrating the example of sales tactics employed by toy companies during Christmas to boost their sales after the occasion as well. When Christmas is fast approaching, toy companies start marketing particular toys to kids so they then persuade their parents to purchase it.

The companies then undersupply toy stores so when the parents visit the stores to make the required purchase, they have made the commitment for the respective toy and when they cannot find it, they have no choice except to visit the store again after December to purchase the required toy. The alternative available to them is to disappoint their kids by taking the inconsistency route, which they do not wish to.

Your job is to ensure you stay consistent in your efforts and leverage this in the behavior of others as well. Here are a few things you can do to manipulate others through the power of consistency.

- First, you always have to make sure you are consistent in your efforts of trying to build rapport with someone, persuading someone, making them like you and then winning them over. Nobody can instantly hand you over the power to control them except for in cases where someone is completely dependent on you or is so weak emotionally that he/she cannot even stand up for his/her basic rights. Otherwise, people with even a moderate level of self-esteem do not allow you to override them. When dealing with such people, you need to slowly move from the point you build familiarity with them to the point you start influencing them. This does take time, but you can definitely shorten the timespan if you consistently make the right efforts and try striking the iron while it is hot. If you are trying to convince your partner to move in with you, be consistent in the way you shower love onto them and keep reminding them of how important they are to you while telling them how you would never pressurize them into doing something they do not want. If you want your boss to grant you a month's paid leave while you are eligible for only 10 day's paid leave, consistently work hard throughout the time that leads to the time when you wish to get the leave and keep putting up your best behavior and effort. When being consistent in your efforts to please someone, try not to go overboard with someone who may not approve of extra diligence and efficiency.

- Throw in a Demand when You Know Someone Cannot Refuse: As stated before, people have an innate need to be consistent in their efforts especially related to a certain routine they are used to or a promise they have already made. So if you know a friend goes to gym every day at 5 pm, and you want her to pick up some stuff from the grocery store next to her gym, ask her for the favor exactly at 4:40 when you know she is ready to leave for her work out. If she is regular with her fitness routine, she is likely not to bail out on that and will not have any solid reason to refuse fulfilling your request.

- Influence People Right After Doing them a Favor: If you are consistently helping out someone or trying to please them, you can use that to trick them into doing favors for you. Right after you have been super nice to someone or did someone a favor, toss in your demand as well. For instance, you create report for your colleague as he requested you too, and you would like him to cover up for you for 2 days so throw in the request right at that point, and he is likely not to say 'no'. Also known as the principle of reciprocation, this rule is based on the popular American idiom,'You scratch my back and I will do yours.' This principle is deep seated in our subconscious and our culture to the extent that we do not even realize how powerful its effects are.

When someone does us a favor, we feel obliged to repay him/ her in the same way or any other way we find convenient for us. Similarly, when you provide for someone in any way, you expect him/her to return you the favor too and even if you do not nurture that expectation, the other person is likely to conform to the distinctive subconscious demand and fulfill it.

A solid example to illustrate this is the distribution of free samples of food or any other good when you walk into a grocery store. Just because you try something for free, even though you know you are not obligated to make a purchase, subconsciously you feel compelled to do so and most of the times if you have liked that free sample, you will buy some quantity of that product.

If you are trying to influence your target market to take a certain call to action, throw in bait by giving them a free offer or discount. Similarly, if you wish for your team to become extra efficient and productive, give them a paid leave right before a big project to energize them and increase their motivation to work harder.

However, if you see someone doing you a favor in exchange for something they would like you to do, make sure to consider their intentions. If their intentions are pure, go with the flow, enjoy the attention and care, and when you feel like, repay them with kindness.

However, if you are involved in a situation, where you are expected to make a purchase or an investment in return for a favor someone did for you, assess whether or not the outcome would benefit you before making the decision. Remember that just as you try to control others at times, people are likely to have some motives associated with you so you need to be careful when handing someone the power to influence you.

- Target their Sweet Spot: If you are aware of someone's soft or weak points, it is best to target them to make them listen to you. For example, if you know your spouse is an empath and cannot see you in pain, ask them to run errands for you when you feel emotionally drained. If you have a colleague who is a control freak, ask him to lead a project the two of you are working on mutually and let him know that is because he is so good at his work. This is likely to pump up his ego and he is likely to take charge.

Employ these tactics very carefully and consistently, and if you use them while targeting the other person's sweet spot, you will definitely achieve your desired outcome. Now let us move on to the next chapter for more useful techniques to deal with people and influence them.

Chapter 5: More Effective Techniques To Influence Others

Along with all the techniques that you have learnt so far, here are a few more, which if you work on committedly will help you achieve the desired results and always achieve success when it comes to manipulating others.

Generate Urgency

To influence, you need to create urgency. Unless you do that, oftentimes, people will not respond as positively as you hope them to. Creating urgency means that you create a scenario or paint a picture of the problem at hand in a manner that it appears as a pressing issue making the other person feel he/she must act as you want. If you want your friend to file for medical insurance, make her feel how urgent that is and how she must not wait another minute to act on it.

Here are some tactics you can use to create urgency in order to manipulate others.

- Ask Probing Questions: Asking the right and often probing questions is just the trick that can help you create earnestness in someone to act as desired. If you are tired of your partner not taking his debt issues seriously, ask questions such as 'What problems are we suffering because of financial issues?', 'What are your concerns about your ever-increasing debt?' and 'Is your debt the reason your self-esteem is dwindling?' Make sure to ask the questions with concern in your tone and facial expressions so the other person feels your apprehension and then becomes stimulated to take the desired action.

- Give Examples: Another effective tactic to create urgency is to illustrate examples of other people who went through similar experiences, and ended up suffering in the end because they failed to take the right action at the right time. If you wish for your best friend going through depression to get therapy instead of staying engulfed in the darkness all alone, talk to him about how another friend went through the same traumatic episode, but recovered soon after because she had a therapist by her side. Reinforce the urgency by talking about the problem and sharing relevant examples.

- Make them Visualize: Visualization is an incredibly effective technique that does not only help you become more invested in your work and put in extra effort to achieve your goals, but also helps you in influencing others as well.

When you wish for someone to oblige to your commands, paint them a beautiful picture of how doing that chore will benefit them. Make them visualize the end outcome and have all their senses involved in the experience so they become fully immersed in the visualization and are then motivated to take the required action.

If you want your students to do well in a certain internship they have signed up for, help them visualize how doing it well will benefit them in the long run and help them land a great job. Make them visualize the sights, sounds, expressions, feelings, sensations and even tastes associated with success. For instance, you can ask them to think of their most favorite ice cream and think of having that when they are successful. Similarly, you can make them think of the sound the ATM makes when your money is about to come out and how you would hear those sounds and feel the touch of crisp dollar bills when you land a fantastic, well paid job.

When you make someone completely involved in an imagination, it targets and influences their subconscious and imbeds relevant suggestions in it. When your subconscious mind becomes focused on a certain outcome, it then makes you work towards achieving that outcome.

- Pinpoint the Scarcity: Earnestness can easily be created by using the principle of scarcity. If you want someone to oblige to your demands, let them know how a certain thing is scarce or an offer is only available for a limited time. For instance, if you wish your friend to apply for a scholarship grant for her M.Phil thesis as soon as possible, let her know how the offer ends in 2 days and how she will miss out on a wonderful opportunity by missing it out. If you want your friends to go out on a food festival with you, inform them of how it ends tonight and how all of you will miss a lifetime experience if you do not go today.

While creating urgency, try not to force the other person into doing something. People who are smart enough to realize this tactic are likely to feel offended by it and then distance themselves from you for a while. Thus, do employ the tactics, but very cautiously so people do not feel upset by anything.

Be Aware of Your BATNA

BATNA refers to your 'best alternative to a negotiated agreement' and is your preferred fallback option that you resort to when things do not go, as you want. It is different from the bottom line, which refers to a fixed position that limits the options available to you and keeps you from discovering new actions.

Knowing your BATNA means that you think through a certain situation to come up with different scenarios wherein things do not happen as desired and then opt for a settlement that appeals to you the most. You need to assess the different alternatives available to you and then opt for the most promising substitute that suits you the most.

If, however, you begin negotiation with a bottom line in your demand, you are likely not to explore any other promising options and may have to settle only for it if the negotiations do not go through as planned. Let us share with you an example to explain this better.

If you are trying to get your charity program funded by some big MNC's and are in talks with a few potential sponsors, you need to begin with asking for complete 100% sponsorship that includes every aspect of the event. Your plan B can be to cut it down by 10% or by eliminating one activity from the package instead of asking for only 50% funds as soon as the sponsors reject your initial proposal. If you present different alternatives, it is likely you can get 70% funds and some added benefits instead of just settling for a small amount of funds.

Similarly, if you wish for a colleague to help you out with a project, give him different options instead of withdrawing your request or asking him to do just a little bit if the first initial request of help is unacceptable to him.

Always be aware of your BATNA and present it in an interesting way while offering benefits of doing that to the concerned individual.

Make Use of Objective Criteria

When trying to persuade someone to carry out a certain task, make use of objective criteria. Settle on a framework based on objective criteria using facts, figures, statements and underlying interests, needs, goals and opinions.

For instance, while having an interdepartmental discussion in the company regarding the launch event of a new service, you become quite convinced that you need to rush it to the market as soon as you can. Now if you wish for the entire team to understand that, you need to provide evidence in form of marketing data and tie it in with how all the team members will benefit from incentives and promotions if the launch goes as planned and receives an overwhelmingly positive response as desired.

When choosing objective criteria for a certain matter, take into consideration factors such as market value, legal standards, contractual terms, mission and objectives, vision and other factors according to the nature of the problem.

Be the Authority on the Matter

People like listening and following someone they perceive as an authority figure. If you wish for others to listen to you attentively and dance to your tune, you need to come off as an authority figure on a certain subject matter. If you want someone to take action against physical abuse and end the vicious cycle of codependency she/he is involved in, tell her/him how you have been through the same or dealt with people who underwent that trauma and how putting an end to that pain is crucial for their betterment right now.

To be an authority, you need to have command over the topic and be fully aware of the ins and outs related with it so you have complete knowledge on the issue and can convince others about it easily. If you want your business partner to buy certain software for your small business, become convinced about it first and use your knowledge about it to persuade him then.

Carry out an in depth research on the issue to collect as much data on it as possible and then study it on your own to brush your knowledge of it. It is only when you are well versed on it that you can share it with others, educate others about it and influence them in the desired manner.

Bring in the Element of Empathy

Empathy never goes to waste and always does the trick of winning people over. When being empathetic towards people, remember not to do it just to fulfill your ulterior motives. Empathy is about feeling the pain of others as your own and is something so beautiful that it needs to be incorporated positively in all your actions.

Be your compassionate, loving self with others and be as empathetic as you can with people you genuinely care about. Feel the pain of others, be around them to show your support and do not push anyone to do something he/she feels uncomfortable about. You will build a fantastic rapport with people once you become empathetic towards them and this will only make it easier for you to inspire them.

Remember the Names and Faces of People

An effective way to shower attention on someone especially someone you have only met once or twice is to remember their face and name. People love to build connection with others and when they do, they quickly feel drawn towards that very person. When you meet someone, ask his/her name and use it a couple of times during the conversation so you imbed it in your subconscious mind. Also, pick any prominent facial feature and tie it with that person's name so you remember it easily.

The next time you meet him/her, greet him/her using their name affectionately and it will definitely cheer him/her up drawing them towards you.

Try to make written notes of all the practices you try and how each works out in your favor. Certain tactics work well with certain people while some don't. Therefore, write down about how you implement each tactic so you can keep track of your performance and improve on it the next time.

Conclusion

We have come to the end of the book. Thank you for reading and congratulations for reading until the end.

I hope this book helps you build a charming personality that draws others towards you and makes you influence them.

Do You Like My Book & Approach To Publishing?

If you like my writing and style and would love the ease of learning literally everything you can get your hands on from Fantonpublishers.com, I'd really need you to do me either of the following favors.

1: First, I'd Love It If You Leave a Review of This Book on Amazon.

2: Check Out My Emotional Mastery Books

Note: This list may not represent all my Keto diet books. You can check the full list by visiting my author page.

[Emotional Intelligence: The Mindfulness Guide To Mastering Your Emotions, Getting Ahead And Improving Your Life](#)

[Stress: The Psychology of Managing Pressure: Practical Strategies to turn Pressure into Positive Energy (5 Key Stress Techniques for Stress, Anxiety, and Depression Relief)](#)

[Failure Is Not The END: It Is An Emotional Gym: Complete Workout Plan On How To Build Your Emotional Muscle And Burning Down Anxiety To Become Emotionally Stronger, More Confident and Less Reactive](#)

Subconscious Mind: Tame, Reprogram & Control Your Subconscious Mind To Transform Your Life

Body Language: Master Body Language: A Practical Guide to Understanding Nonverbal Communication and Improving Your Relationships

Shame and Guilt: Overcoming Shame and Guilt: Step By Step Guide On How to Overcome Shame and Guilt for Good

Anger Management: A Simple Guide on How to Deal with Anger

Get updates when we publish any book that will help you master your emotions: http://bit.ly/2fantonpubpersonaldevl

To get a list of all my other books, please fantonwriters.com, my author central or let me send you the list by requesting them below: http://bit.ly/2fantonpubnewbooks

3: Grab Some Freebies On Your Way Out; Giving Is Receiving, Right?

I gave you a complimentary book at the start of the book. If you are still interested, grab it here.

5 Pillar Life Transformation Checklist: http://bit.ly/2fantonfreebie

www.ingramcontent.com/pod-product-compliance
Lightning Source LLC
Chambersburg PA
CBHW050841040426
42333CB00058B/392